The Blinding Light Circling Elpida, in one act

Dina Kafiris

original plus

this collection 'The Blinding Light Circling Elpida, in one act'
first published in Britain by
'original plus'
17 High Street
Maryport
Cumbria.   CA15 6BQ

https://sites.google.com/site/samsmiththejournal/
smithsssj@aol.com

ISBN 978-0-9570197-7-5

cover photograph by Dina Kafiris

printed by original plus press

Acknowledgements
Versions of some poems here have previously appeared in
American, British and Canadian Studies, *The Glasgow Review,*
Horizon Review, and *The Recusant;* and in Greek in *Nea Synteleia*

For my father.

Contents

The Blinding Light
Circling Elpida,
in one act

The Mistress

She,

Grand hostess of tongue-twisted lies, found comfort in this Art Deco
gem – a small café dripping with intimacy, chattering lips,
momentary pauses from working actors, writers of the exquisite and
bohemian kind who congregated within its closed doors.

A historian, as she was known amongst the staff, singlehandedly
turned this haunt into a butcher's kitchen. Because of her, the
beloved Mr P, favoured as the next Nobel Laureate, stopped writing;
a minister, name not mentioned, left her husband for his secretary to
spite him; Mr M, opening night, on his way to the theatre, caught his
wife canoodling in the corner of the same café, with his own brother,
rumoured to have fled to a monastery far from the glory of the stage.

'I'm no different from a social columnist,' she once exclaimed.
'I report the facts. A noble service for my fellow man.'

Ear to the wall, who would dare repeat her discoveries without
permission.

She screened faces belonging to the withered and the unspoilt as
they entered her slaughterhouse, thrust away from the winter's glare.
Became she did, a witness to the mention of a name, sound of a kiss,
explosions of laughter, whispers in corners hidden from the human
stare (so they thought). She knew very well there existed secrets in
every peck, each exchanged word, each message left on a mobile
phone. Whilst Piaf's 'Les Amants de Teruel' played, lost behind the
babble of voices, her leering look cautioned them.

But as scenarios continued to unravel, the cigarette hanging from her
painted lips loosened, dry from the cold she so despised, exhaling
smoke over the copy of *Henry and June*, given by HER.

She stretched out a plump leg having noticed a ladder in her stockings – piano keys scaling up her inner thigh – where her lover's fingers had travelled the night before. Through fake auburn curls she caught the lingering eye of the man beside her. With no smile to offer, she concentrated on finishing her third coffee, slowly, ever so slowly, interrupted by thoughts of HER.

The woman who had promised her wildflowers from the Grampians, mud baths in Turkey, to sail the rivers of Myanmar...

Who would have imagined, Madeleine de la Rosa had a mistress.

Nostalgia

In walks uncertainty. The disorientated anarchist. Her sculptured crown swamped with dreadlocks. Asks for directions. A harem of eyes study her. She amuses some. No glances are met. They return to their conversations. Gaze at the entrance to the café. More absent expressions flock inside. Away from the season's bitter hold. They seek the warmth inside. Reminiscing the lost summer. The smell of heat. Sun against their faces. It paints their frozen lips. Outside fumes smother the city. Cars crawl around the square. Motorbikes mount the pavements. Drivers throw their anger to the one in front. Pedestrians await the traffic lights. Stern faces. Pale. Pierced. Tattooed. Couples grasp each other. They kiss. The cold creeps by. Naked trees pose as the city bathes in its dread. One fears the days to come.

Hypocrisy Has A Face

You claim truths which are unreliable,
Facts that are no doubt fictional,
Embrace fabrications as if true,
Disregard details that exist as evidence,
Censor with the intention of falsifying history,
Since truth makes you a traitor, a martyr, a victim.

That is to say, you lie to exist.

Café Corais, Athens, September 29th 2007

You Left Leaving

I love thee
though you are gone
Now, free to wander.

I love thee
praise the restless seas, *a destiny's misfortune*
fleeing into my embrace
(Salty taste left on the mouth)

I love thee
poetry from a land you left
translate in each glance
(Stroking dry fingers on perfumed skin)

I love thee
a tone too dark to be greeted
I stand in the church without you
(Grasping a photograph and creased letter)

I love thee
youths dye rocks with your blood
head under steel toe boot, *tattoos identity*
(Waiting for that phone call)

Another Day

A silk shirt wrinkles
on the living room floor,
next to a pile of *Athens News*.
It's that time after work
when the cat purrs.
NET News is about to start.
She unzips a tailored skirt,
soon to climb the stairs,
open the bedroom door;
but till then, her shadow
is examined through the curtain.

Meeting of the Holy Synod

The day he departed
with an early morning pause,

the mountains that bounded Athens
were silenced by incessant snowfall,
wayward rivers ran mercilessly
washing faith in all directions,
rolling clouds confiscated the light,
thunder pined through the gloomy skies,
twice striking the human ear.

Braving the cold,
emos, desperate for another Messiah,
rallied at the steps of the church
in black jeans, patched by anxious mothers,
debuting new faces stripped of piercings;
their shivering bodies and gritted teeth, ignored.

But believers understood,
that when the trumpets blew
to announce that a preacher had entered,
and the existing hour was brought to a halt,
that they were now without a shepherd.

Rebirth

Flowers began to blossom in our tiny village,
the morning he arrived – that white dove.
Rejoicing in spirit, we laughed,
our hearts bursting with love.

In His Memory

Amazed how *he* could have done it
Forgive them in that way

Was she supposed to take pity on
the baker who deprived her of change,
the boss for giving the job to his niece,
the husband who bedded her sister...

The beggar, pocketing twenty pounds,
prayed for pardon, before nailing her to the wall,
arms pointed at the heavens

to know *his* pain

A man whose heart was far greater
than her own.

Playing God
for Nanos Valaoritis

A momentous occasion/ that blank screen/

you meet again like old friends/ face to face/ no ostracising/ no games/
just pure unabridged fiction/ you're loyal that way/ hoping the words
will appear without your contribution/ for a story to unravel in front of
your very eyes/ you welcome the thought/ consider the possibilities/
envision the adaptation/ thrilled at the prospect/ the chance to be spared/
liberated from the unbearable sweating and sleepless nights/ ideas
cropping up during that morning beverage/ or when soaking in the
bathtub trying to erase the day's troubles/

nose stuck in the newspaper/ hiding the cigarette that made you an
outcast/ you think back to when your smudged notebook rested by a
mug of coffee and that faithful packet/ why must it all change you sigh/
they were the times most favoured/ the days when you wrote epics/
wishing/ once more/ to exhale fiction with the same ease writers
exaggerated in the back rooms of the pubs and cafés/

the silence disturbs you/ sickly nostalgic for the sound of your old
typewriter/ a computer knows only how to whisper/ *tap-tap tap-tap*/ you
believe that words are not earned when fingers do not ache/ surprisingly
it pleases you/ no more arthritis or doctors' bills/ nevertheless/ you are
saddened/ for the intimacy has vanished/ the words don't carry their
weight/ before the infinite word counted/ before you thought of each one
meticulously/ before the ink pressed them on paper/ key after key/ now
there are many/ lines full of words/ effortlessly deleted/ copied/ cut and
pasted/ you want your words to be felt/ a muted keyboard suggests
secrets/ you write for it to be read out loud/ shouted over the Thames/
you have nothing to hide/ which is why you want your laptop to scream
obscenities/ for the writing has to acquire movement/ so that the
characters journey through the story/ you grow susceptible to their every
whim/ you have not learnt to betray/ (not up to now)/ a victim of your
characters' flaws/ you reinvent yourself within the body of the text/

a writer beckons for a breath/ struggling to separate their life from
the imaginary other/ the reality doesn't seem so satisfying/
wondering who has stolen whose life/ you or your protagonist/ what
does it matter/ you are indisputably alive/ breathing aspirations/
unfaithful to persons walking in and out of your study/ regretfully/
you don't budge/ you can't/ since what you have in front of you is a
far greater gift/ the truest gift/ a soul's turbulent adventure/ your
creation/ how exhilarating/ to be able to compose in a way that
prevents others saying what they wish to but fear to/ you/ a master
of letters/ leaves them vulnerable/ searching for themselves in the
unbound manuscript/ afraid that their weaknesses have been
recorded/ as you are a witness to their being/ though your
fascination lies further than the familiar/ they are of no interest/ it is
the woes of strangers that have caught your fancy/ faithfully
following their shadows/ footsteps/ what their hands have touched/
you are driven by their discretion(s)/ vulnerabilities/ you compile
motives for their actions/

weeks and months race by/ your final draft is ready to leave the
room/ come up against the critics/ when it reaches other hands/ it is
seen differently/ on occasions not appreciated/ underestimated/
opinionated men dictate what you can and can't say/ and how you
should say it/ in other words/ the way in which to express yourself/
they question the experiments with narrative style/ the tendentious
tone/ nationalistic sentiment/ your dogmatic approach/ they stand
confident/ trends change/ you grin/ as you pass the private clubs
where your name has been mentioned/ yet you obey/

You become a brand/ an enterprise/ named the next Beckett/ Joyce/
it all becomes impersonal/ what happened to the literary endeavour/
when did your 'pen' start to imitate your contemporaries/ or scholars
from public schools start meddling with the anarchists of the
fictional page/ hadn't their predecessors judged unfairly in the past/
when masterpieces found themselves lost amongst a slush pile/ that
was when small printing houses were more courageous/ when
movements evolved/ schools of writers were established/ surely/
how can they know what they themselves have not executed/ so

adamant to judge the unfamiliar/ read they say/ it's all in the reading/ you refer to them as parasites/ the outsiders/ the men who could never write that one accomplished novel/ gleaming with eagerness to tarnish the ones who dared/ and succeeded/ asserting power without hesitation or guilt/

regardless/ your salvation rests in the readers/ you wrote it for Them/ you/ the storyteller in search of an audience/ it needed to be said/ which is why/ impatiently/ you wait/ grateful for some feedback/ to confirm whether you had done right/ introduced some kind of justice/ for your main character/ for yourself/ so that when leaving your house every morning you'd feel assured that you chose well/ that you let your protagonist go without remorse/ freeing yourself from responsibility/ finally able to return to the life of a recluse/ ready to confront the new idea waiting for a beginning.

Faith

A baby's wailing charges through the aisles,
gurgling trickles of holy water between immersions,
supported by unfamiliar hands, paddles like a fish.
The priest's fumbling fingers seek the scissors,
snipping four locks of uncut hair, crosswise,
whilst the hundred bear witness.

Friends, Indeed!

I feel free Madame Bloom; the Northern wind has cleansed me.

You kneel before sculpted flowers, eager to recreate a village
seen through skimmed postcards by a sender you wished to ignore.

I, on the other hand, forgot to water mine,
last year's Christmas present – shrivelled like prunes.
Funny, it was as if you'd expected it.
Yet you didn't utter a word. I've come to accept
that you've been silenced by a genocide you rarely mention.

To you my lady I am faithful, a fact you can't deny.
Pleasing you with my bourgeois ways and discreet departures.

Unexpected that Southern wind, knocked me to the ground.

An omen. I'm sure you'll agree.

In Giving

Give me love,

I will give you bread and water to calm a bellowing gut
that despairs over rumours of drought.

Give me books,

I will give you clothes to comfort weather-beaten bones
bruised by the cold bite that grinds humour dry.

Give me music and dance,

I will give you soap to scrub tired hands gashed by a barren soil
that once fed a village mocked for their jolly bellies.

Give me art,

I will give you local beauty, a muse excused from love,
bartered in a bar brawl to fill a father's empty pockets.

Give me a bed,

I will give you visions to nurture a starving imagination
wounded by the isolation of a land and its apocalypse.

Athens, Greece   18/9/08

The Blinding Light Circling Elpida, in one act

[Evening. Central Athens.
Backstage at the theatre. Elpida's dressing room.
An hour before the curtain goes up, Alexandra approaches Elpida,
concerned about her actions. Elpida appears distressed.]
Time – Present

Elpida, what are you doing?
You as my witness can surely answer that, my dear Alexandra.
This is what worries me, that my sight deceives me.
I am brushing my hair, you senile woman.
But my sweet girl, they shaved it off. Remember?
I know that. Do you think I am mad, or that I have forgotten?
Do you?
[She pauses.]
He has to have heard my prayers. Has he not?
What sort of a question is that? Of course he has.
If only I could see him, hear his thoughts.
If only he would grant me the opportunity to discuss my options,
so that I can ask where I went wrong.
Wouldn't that be marvellous?
But I have faith, do you hear? Faith! Even though...
What alternative do I have? A beggar's choices are little or none.
Faith is all that remains.
It gives me the courage to get through each day with dignity.
So I have decided that I must go on as usual.
Nothing will change, do you hear?
Every morning, I will sit in front of that mirror and brush my hair:
a hundred strokes for a hundred prayers that this will all go away.
Yes, I have made up my mind.
I have decided that I am not going to waste
what little strength I have dwelling on what if.
Hear! Hear!

[Alexandra dances around the dressing room
with a wine glass in her hand.
Several times she loses her balance
when one foot clumsily treads on the other.
Meanwhile, Elpida drops her robe in front of the mirror.
The truth of evolution is evident in her reflection.
She puts on the theatrical costume ready for her final performance.]
The last few nights on stage,
I saw my mother in the front row,
shedding tears of joy.
In her hand, she held the handkerchief I had bought;
it was a gift for her birthday.
She was my only audience,
and I, the only performer on that stage.
She watched in admiration, listened intently.
Then she gave me an approving grin.
I remember that smile.
She had not stopped smiling that particular smile
since that memorable day:
the day the dictatorship collapsed.
She threw herself at my father and cried the same tears of joy,
saying again and again,
'We're free, Aristotle.
We're finally free from those barbarians.
Are you listening? We've been liberated!'
She grabbed my father's hand, lifting him to his feet,
twirled him around the room,
the same way you were twirling,
shouting at the top of her voice,
'We're free! We're free!'
I have played that scene repeatedly in my head
so that I would never forget her smile.
The year she fell ill, sadness overwhelmed her,
and that smile was lost.
But mankind will always be enslaved,
either by government, or by health.
We, as Greeks, have always been a condemned race.
But proud and brave – we must never ignore that fact.
This is why you must fight like a hero, as you have in the past.

Do you hear me?

I hear you, God. I hear you.

Elpida, it was me. It was me who was talking to you.

Who did you think it was? Who were you speaking to?

The miracle I was waiting for.

Life once more is answering my pleas.

A great soldier always dies a hero. Is that not what you once said?

But you're one of our country's national heroes,

my beautiful Elpida.

Courageous and important on both stages:

as a leading actress, and as a woman.

[Elpida lifts her glass to propose a toast.]

Long live the freedom of companionship!

Long live the freedom to love!

And, long live the comforts of our motherland, my compatriot!

[They clink glasses.]

To our history!

To deliverance!

And let's not forget the most important. To good health!

[They raise their glasses once again.]

From your mouth to God's ear.

CURTAIN

[End]

Café Cinque, Sydney   18/5/2009

The Column

La Torre Pendente di Pisa, failed to stand vertically.
Specialists blamed this on its poor foundations.
Her column followed a different school of thought;
a pillar whose strength rivalled that of the Pentelic marble,
yet suffered considerable damage from a playground mishap.

Unlike Frida, she picked up the pen,
employing a battalion of words,
imprints of a lost childhood, abundant phrases
feuding backbiting tongues and discourteous stares:
'A curse of the illiterate,' her mother swore.
For a while she walked on stilts, transforming flatties
to freaks in a touring sideshow;
crayons and felt tips coloured in kingdoms, distant lands
where she subdued the sanctimonious drivel of princesses,
secured the admiration of knights and kings, sentenced traitors,
consoled peasants, adhered to the teachings of ancient prophets –
here her pagan eyes were compared to flawless emeralds.
Boredom helped create a world
where she was permitted to intervene,
but even this distraction could not protect her from the fisted hand
striving on paper to bow to the one reality,
that she, like the tower, might topple.
Frequent rendezvous with Hippocrates's 'disciples' displeased her,
morning breaths unkindly met; meticulous sculptors
strapping her torso with bandages, fitting her for a bespoke corset –
the smell of drying plaster repeatedly made her gut churn.
So she shut her eyes, migrated to a self far from the common folk
where her beauty equalled Helen of Troy's and Lady Guinevere's,
reflecting on whether Waterhouse would have been as kind
as he was in his depiction of 'Circe Poisoning the Sea'.
'Beauty is only skin deep,' her father promised,
barely in school uniform
when the pointing of fingers persecuted her.
As a pupil, she walked hopeful,

having learnt that the skill of writing could make her notable.
Her scribbled notes spoke of society and the perils of women;
she refused to accept that the plight of Austen,
Woolf, Plath ... went unrewarded.

Her column would be restored. Now a swan in a crowd,
she followed the gift inspired by a prolific imagination,
she crossed into the real world where she'd gaze
from the decks of ships, from port to port,
out of plane windows that carried her across
the unkempt and barren landscapes of foreign continents.
In these adopted hometowns, she would be compensated,
taken aback by the rewards bestowed upon the future:
an illustrious history of literary garlands,
accolades that firmly established her reputation
as a distinguished woman of letters.
'The pen in time forgives all,' she said at a news conference.
These words forced scholars into the donated archive
of a university library,
scavenging for truths, frustrated at their inability
to decode the wit that had eased her journey,
fictional oeuvre that served as a testimony to the stone years.

Bangor, Wales   22/7/2010

Tree of Misfortune

It was inevitable that the sentiment of love
would fade from the widow's eyes,
the harm inflicted upon her was irreparable
once sorrow put down roots
and buried the loss in the core of the cortex,
allowing the deceased to resurface
at her beck and call.

Circumstance transformed a character
the locals spoke fondly of
into a woman whose grief had overtaken her,
and rightly so.
Daily, she fought to hold onto
the measly portions of affection that still persisted
to prevent her turning into a dying animal
feasting on the disappointments of others,
seeking pleasure from the wounded.
For this reason alone, she was understandably excused
when outbursts of uncontrollable resentment
poured out of this housewife collapsed in her chair,
perched like a statue where time, expression, and goodwill,
had been simultaneously frozen.
She despised all when her dearest Emmanuel was taken ill,
not long after he was made redundant from a job
he had remained committed to right to the last day.
'A shortage of doctors,' staff explained,
cautious about offering expressions of sympathy
to this grandmother who had anticipated retirement
with her loving husband.
She had planned to accompany him to Meganisi,
his childhood playground,
a secret peering through the hidden curtains of Lefkada:
the island where music metamorphosed into words
that balanced like thirsty leeches on poets' lips,
words that enticed skilful and willing hands to record
histories, tragedies, and prophetic visions.

The countryside grew damper after his premature farewell;
it stopped the anguished wife
from speaking further neighbourly words.
How disheartening the economic crisis was to the romantic,
and to the optimist who imagined a different horizon,
with the passing of each falling star exhaling the sky.

Nea Penteli, Athens   *6/10/10*

Afterword

From Nea Penteli comes the news

Of a kind of writing that combines the silence of the age old landscape with the chatter of fiery tongues ceaselessly talking 4000 years ago until now without stopping even for a drink of Raki… these poetic notes record and transmit what the ears think they have been hearing all the time although this is not necessarily true.

She scribbled notes and spoke of society…now a swan in a crowd… then the perils of women …going together in the Tsar's ballroom…fatal for Seneca Tolstoi in the railway station…and the duel that wiped the blackboard clean of Siniavski, Pushkin and Poliakoff…what colours on the walls of writing resplendent in the twilight of letters and numbers …who knows how long ago was the eternal universe some claim is finite…repetition will everywhere claim its victims, …what 's the cost of a kiss in the Levant, "the Married woman's four the Widow's twice five and four and the Unmarried Maiden's one thousand golden florins"…EAST WEST ACROSS THE BRAZEN SEA…sailed the intrepid word bringing news to the untrodden shores…where were you all my life…? when fingers pointed towards the guilty and the innocent …hiding among the trees the couple copulated for the face lift of the population of elves yes and dwarfs and giants…treacherously romantic Guinevere …when words would again acquire their connection to things … the house on the hill inhabited by ideas …and remakes brand new barely in school uniform …stepping over the Rose of the winds… Athens small and walled in ottoman times.

Thinking writing would make her Roman…strapped in bandages like Frida Kahlo… the good and the evil… age old twins… the eastern continent huge and empty…

Who are the Greeks among us…? the geeks in the gulfs of the West… or the Cornish Celts winged and warped by the English to enlist …in the world's facebook…

The velvet gaze meets Dina… and sends her forward in the unchartered seas… of the rising tumultuously Pacific Ocean Okeanus' Ogygias navel island of the hidden fairy Calypso… setting Odysseus free...

Nanos Valaoritis
Athens 17 Febr. 2014

The author

Dina Kafiris was born in Sydney in 1969, of Greek parents. She came to Europe in 1993 and has lived in Greece and Britain. She was a member of the prestigious Corais group of the literary review Nea Synteleia, (New End of the World), under the Greek Surrealist poet Nanos Valaoritis. She is currently completing a PhD in Creative and Critical Writing in Bangor, North Wales.